Two Gentlemen Visit Sri Lanka

A Visit to Colombo and Travel with A Kind Companion

Andrew Sadler

Copyright © Andrew Sadler 2016

All Rights Reserved

No part of this book may be reproduced, stored in a retrieval system, or transmitted, in any form or by any means,

electronic, mechanical, photocopying, recording or otherwise without prior permission of the copyright owner.

The Author assert his moral right to be identified as the authors of this work.

2016

ISBN: 978-0-9569377-6-6

Contents

1. Why we went to Sri Lanka..1

2. Preparation for the Visit..4

3. Arrival at Bandaranaike International Airport and how we found our Kind Companion..9

4. First Day in Colombo. Renuka Hotel, Tea at Galle Face and Dinner with Old Friends..14

5. Day 2. The Fort - Pettah Market - The National Museum - and Dinner with Indranee..18

6. Day 3 Visit to the Cancer Hospital - Mount Lavinia Hotel - Dinner near Independence Square 21

7. Day 4 Relaxation at Mount Lavinia -. A Walk on the Beach..28

8. Day 5 Upset Stomach after Buffet - Exploration of Old Haunts - A Train Ride and Dinner at the Golf Club.............29

9. Day 6 Sigiriya & Reacquaintance with Ishan our Kind Companion..32

10. Day 7 Sigiriya to Kandy and a visit to the Queens Hotel 36

11. Day 8 Teaching Hospital Kandy, Eric's Injury, Peradeniya University & Botanical Gardens............................39

12. Day 9 Tea Factory, Nuwara Eliya, the Hill Club and Grand Hotel..44

13. Day 10 Ella in the Hill Country...48

14. Day 11. Ella and the Trains...51

15. Day 12. Hill Country Ella to Unawatuna Beach Resort. 53

16. Day 13. Galle, the Dutch Fort and Back to Mount Lavinia...57

17. Day 14. Another Day at Mount Lavinia............................60

18. Day 15. Home..62

19. Appendix 1 Why you should not drive in Sri Lanka.......63

20. Appendix 2 Accounts..65

Images.

No travelogue would be complete without colour images of the places visited. In order to reduce the cost of the printed book and to make reading more convenient for the Kindle book the images are omitted and are posted at:

www.twoinlanka.co.uk

1. Why we went to Sri Lanka

I had often thought that I would return to Sri Lanka someday.

In 1994 I had spent three months working at the National Cancer Hospital at Maharagama, which is near Colombo, and subsequently three weeks travelling around the country with my wife Maralyn and our two children.

My original invitation to go to Sri Lanka was the responsibility of the late Dr Anthony Gabriel who was the senior surgeon there. Dr Gabriel had spent some time in England during his training, as had his father, who was also a Sri Lankan surgeon married to an English nurse.

At the time of my previous visit I had just completed my training as an Oral and Maxillofacial Surgeon and was about to take up my position as a consultant in the speciality in Lincolnshire. During my training in London, Oral & Maxillofacial Surgeons were in competition with Ear Nose and Throat and Plastic Surgeons for the surgical treatment of mouth cancer; this diluted the clinical experience for us trainees. Thus the reason for my going to Maharagama was to increase my surgical experience as they had a large number of mouth cancers. This considerable workload was caused by the habit of chewing pann which consisted of betel leaves with areca nut, slaked lime and tobacco wrapped within them. The habit was to chew this and hold it within the cheek; this was supposed to have health benefits and gave a buzz from the release of alkaloids through the lining of the mouth. However it also caused cancers within the cheek.

At that time there was a requirement for Sri Lankan trainees to spend a year abroad before they took up their definitive positions and this led to several coming to work in our department in Lincolnshire, one of whom remained permanently as an Associate Specialist.

At the time of my visit to the Cancer Hospital the senior trainee there was Panduka Jayasekera. Now 22 years later he is one of their senior surgeons. Panduka spent a year in the UK soon after I returned working at the Royal Marsden Hospital in London, and I saw him several times during his stay although I was living in Lincoln, 150 miles north of London.

In December 2014 Panduka visited London with a friend and we had dinner at my home in Bow. He asked me then when I was coming back to Sri Lanka. It had always been an ambition in the back of my mind but it was not until that autumn that I decided I would go in 2016, towards the beginning of the year before the monsoon started.

Having decided on February as the month to go I mentioned it to my friend Eric Bell who is a retired Dental Surgeon from Lincoln if he would be interested in accompanying me. I thought it might be of interest to him as he was fond of travelling, interested in Medicine and Dentistry and had not been to Asia before.

I was intending to visit the cancer hospital and also the dental teaching hospital in Peradeniya where all my Sri Lankan visitors to our Oral and Maxillofacial Department in Lincoln had received their undergraduate training. In 2011 I had met Professor W.M.Tilakaratne (known as Tilak) while he was visiting the Royal London Hospital Dental Institute as a visiting Professor of Oral Pathology to Queen Mary University where I was teaching. I had written a chapter for his book 'Oral Medicine and Pathology- A Guide to Diagnosis and Management'. Tilak was now the Dean of the Faculty of Dental Sciences at Peradeniya University. I hoped to visit there.

I also wanted to catch up with Dr P Samaraweera (known as Sam). Sam had been one of the Dental Trainees at the Cancer Hospital when I was there. He had subsequently spent a year at Mount Vernon Hospital, Northwood in 1996 and I had seen him several times during that year. Sam had visited us in Lincoln and when his family came over they visited us at our home in Malvern. Sam had subsequently worked at the University of Peradeniya, teaching anatomy, and also in Dental Practice.

Indranee Amarasinghe was a Consultant at the Cancer Hospital while I was there, and she had been to London once since my visit but for only a few weeks and we had had dinner. She had retired from work in the Cancer Hospital but still worked in the private sector and still lived in the same house in Colombo where I had been for dinner all those years ago. I wanted to see her.

So it was that in January 2016 I finally made the arrangements to re-visit Sri Lanka. I was looking forward to seeing these old friends, seeing the hospital and seeing the changes in the country. I was planning a tour from Colombo to Kandy and travel south to Nuwara Eliya in the Hill Country before going to the south coast and Galle, partly retracing the route I had made with my family at the end of my visit 22 years before.

2. Preparation for the Visit.

A quick search on Skyscanner confirmed that the only airline to fly direct from London to Colombo was Sri Lankan Airlines. We could have saved some money if we had elected to change planes or have a stop en route but we were not prepared to do this. The cheapest flights were through a link to a travel agent from Skyscanner. However I had recently read a newspaper report about a booking which had been made twice from no fault of the passenger and no one, neither Skyscanner, the intermediary agent nor the airline would accept responsibility. I had also read that this agent had asked for extra money from a passenger and that the quoted price was not fixed but was only a promise to try and get that rate when the small print was analysed.

I contacted Flightbookers as they had been recommended by a friend. They seemed quite helpful at first and I spoke at some length to a lady on the telephone who called me after my initial contact by email. She wanted to book us a tour but I did not want that as I wanted to make sure I saw my old friends and visited the hospital before planned our travelling; having failed to sell us a tour they lost interest and failed to call us back with an airfare quote as they had promised.

Trialfinders, who had been helpful for an Australian trip quoted us an expensive airfare. We therefore booked directly from the Sri Lankan Airlines web site. This was slightly more expensive than the cheap quote from the dodgy agency via Skyscanner but it did have the facility to show flights at different times and days around the preferred travel time so you could pick the cheapest.

I then consulted the UK government web site for advice as well as the Lonely Planet guide. An ETA (electronic transport authority) is required to visit Sri Lanka. It is not necessary to get it beforehand as you can buy a visa on arrival but it is cheaper and very easy to buy it online before departure for 35 USD; this also saves you a queue on arrival.

We looked for health advice. It is no longer necessary to take Malaria prophylaxis as the risk is too small to justify it in the north of the country and non-existent in the south. There is a risk of Dengue Fever so it is advisable to keep mosquitos away and the recommended method is to cover yourself up, use mosquito nets at night, if the room is not sealed, and spray yourself and clothes (with natural fibres) with DEET (N,N- diethylmetatoluamide). It comes in various strengths 50% giving the longest protection. It should be applied to the face by wiping it on with the hands. We bought three cans of 50% DEET from a supermarket at home (Trade Name: Jungle Formula). Two cans would have been enough for the two of us for two weeks.

We took sun screen factor 50. DEET should be re-applied on top of sunscreen. Lower factor sunscreens can be partly inactivated by DEET. Those of us involved in health care know that sun screen is often not applied in sufficient quantities to give optimal protection and that even if it is it does not protect against all the wavelengths and the best way to avoid skin cancer and premature wrinkling is to keep out of the sun.

A fold up umbrella is useful, more for keeping the sun off than for use in the rain, and I took a hat to keep the sun off my head but found the umbrella best. I applied copious quantities of sun screen to my ears because I know that squamous cancers of the ears can recur as metastatic lesions years after the original primary has been treated and that sun bathing is an absolute no no as even one burning can risk a malignant melanoma in later life.

We were advised to take a sewing kit to repair any mosquito net we used if it had holes in it but this was never used. We only stayed in one hotel in mosquito areas which did not have sealed rooms and the mosquito net was good.

Upset stomach is a complication of change of diet and hygiene. On my previous visit I had suffered this in the first few weeks. Typically this consisted of diarrhoea which came on within a few hours of eating, lasting only a few hours and was without pain or discomfort. Loperamide was very useful before so I bought two packets from the supermarket (Trade name: Imodium). We were advised to drink only bottled water and avoid uncooked food, salad and ice. Bottled water was available everywhere and provided complimentary in most of the hotel rooms.

We took enough clothes for two weeks including shirts with long sleeves to keep the insects off us and some warm clothes as we were planning to visit the hill country which we knew can be chilly and even cold at night. Warm clothes are also desirable in air conditioned restaurants etc.

We wanted to stay in Colombo long enough to see friends so I booked two nights at the Renuka Hotel which is a small modern hotel in Kollupitiya, Colombo 3, almost in the centre of town. I had not stayed there before but had eaten in the restaurant years ago. I figured that as the Renuka was in town and on the busy Galle Road it would be noisy so after we had been there two days we would be better served by staying at the Mount Lavinia Hotel for three nights which is situated on the beach just south of Colombo with easy travelling into town. I made these bookings on booking.com and hotels.com. In the event both hotels were very satisfactory and neither as expensive as many of the high end hotels in Colombo. I did get stomach upset on the first two night after we ate at the buffet in the Mount Lavinia but this was mild and lasted only a few hours so I would not avoid staying there again on this account, Eric was unaffected.

I had originally intended to hire a car for our tour. I emailed a car hire company who advised me not to drive but to hire a car and driver. I had read that it was better to hire a car and driver and had been advised by both my friend in Lincoln (who had recently been home to Sri Lanka for a visit) and Panduka that it was best not to drive oneself. The car hire company sent me a document explaining why I should not drive (see appendix 1) so I decided to take this advice. One other reason was that all the car hire brokers on line were quoting that a 3000 Euro deposit would be required from my credit card. I was concerned that this might disappear as a result of fraud or that if I was involved in a collision I would spend a couple of days sorting it out and getting police forms to claim on the insurance back home.

Eric was concerned that we had not made bookings for the whole trip but I wanted the flexibility. The car hire man wanted me to book a car and driver straight away and I suspected that he realised that I would get other better offers at the airport (which we did). However, I did book a car from the airport to transfer to the Renuka Hotel and paid 36 USD on-line. A mistake as you will see later.

As with all overseas trips some reading about your destination is advisable. I read my diaries from 22 years before and both Eric and I bought copies of the most recent Lonely Planet guide which I highly recommend.

In addition I bought two travelogues on my Kindle which I commend to visitors; both were concerned with recent visits. 'Sri Lanka Diaries 75 Tips to help plan your trip - A Couple's Travel Journal' by Cedric Loiselle and Sarah Carighan was written by a young Canadian couple who had been living in Thailand. The book is an easy ready and full of information on culture and what you can expect if you a travelling on a tight budget. So I would recommend it but note that there are many column inches of moaning particularly how expensive it was which was the opposite of our experience. I expect it was because we were approaching it at a different time of life with different resources or perhaps because they had been living in Thailand where prices were even less than Sri Lanka. Nevertheless at the end of the book they write about their trip very positively and are glad they did it.

'Curious Chronicles from Sri Lanka' by Gavin Anderson is written by a young Englishman who is also careful with his cash but has a more positive outlook. I recommend both these books.

It is not possible to take much Sri Lankan cash into the country and the money exchanges in London therefore do not have it. Many of the prices are quoted to tourists in US Dollars and these are easy to exchange. I therefore took a lot of cash in dollars and changed some at the bank at the airport on arrival. Gavin in 'Curious Chronicles' warned that out of Colombo and Kandy it might be difficult to pay or get cash on a foreign credit or debit card so I took two belt wallets one (left) for dollars and two cards and one (right) for rupees, two cards and passport.

Gavin writes about the outrage at the cricket match at Galle when the English fans found that they had to pay significantly more to get in than the locals. Be warned this is how it is. When I was there before my European friends referred to it as the 'skin tax'. Dark skin a few rupees, white skin many US Dollars. You just have to accept that the hotels and tourist facilities could not have been built or provided with a budget based on the rupees the locals could afford. The prices are still less than you would pay at home (except for some of the high end hotels), service is excellent and people friendly.

So when is the best time to go? The tourist season runs from November through to March. It seems to be based on travellers from Northern Europe getting away from their cold winters. During this time hotel prices are highest. In May comes the monsoon which is very wet and humid so probably August is a good time to go after the monsoon when the European tourists are not so numerous and hotel prices are lower. However, the Perahera (Buddhist festival) in Kandy in August will raise the prices there to maximum.

Throughout I have quoted prices. At the time one £ bought us 1.41 US Dollars and one USD bought us 141 rupees.

3. Arrival at Bandaranaike International Airport and how we found our Kind Companion

The Sri Lanka Airways flight number UL506 left London Heathrow about half an hour late it was scheduled for 12:35. After an uneventful flight we arrived only five minutes late at Bandaranaike International Airport in Sri Lanka at 4:40 a.m.

The airport seemed very modern and efficient. At 5 a.m. it was buzzing with activity with many flight arrivals. The first thing we had to do was pass through immigration. There was a long queue of people waiting in line to get a visa but we had managed to avoid this, and some extra expense, by getting an ETA (electronic travel authorization) each online before arrival. We had been told that we needed to keep a paper copy of the email we received to say that our application has been approved, however this was not required. The chap on the immigration counter scanned our passports, stamped them and attached a label. We were through.

Once past immigration we were in the duty-free sales area. This was a departure from what we were used to at western airports. For rather than the usual scents, clothing accessories, electronic gadgets and other rubbish there were useful things on sale like washing machines, freezers, refrigerators and cookers. We then proceeded to the baggage hall to collect our cases from the belts. We then we passed customs and found ourselves in the arrivals hall.

The first thing that we saw on arrival was just what we needed, the Bank of Ceylon; there were other banks as well. I changed 240 US dollars into 33900 rupees (an exchange rate of 141.25 Sri Lankan rupees, per US dollar). I had to show my passport and was given a receipt, Eric also changed some money.

The ATM's were hidden further away in the arrivals hall by the coffee shop. When we passed them there was a queue of people waiting to take money. It seemed that changing our

American dollars for rupees at the Bank was much the quickest and most convenient method.

The second thing we needed to do on arrival was to get our telephones fitted with local sim cards. The 'Dialog' counter was the other side of the arrivals hall. A local sim card costs 1,300 rupees, 300 for the card and 1,000 rupees credit. We took our telephones to the counter, handed over the rupees and the fellow fitted sim cards for us. He checked that they were in working order. As with most transactions it appears that if you are a foreigner, you have to produce your passport.

Lastly we needed to find the driver who we had booked for airport transfer to the Renuka Hotel in Colombo. There were a whole bunch of people in the paging area holding boards with the names of people they were supposed to meet, or simply the name of the tour company that they represented. I walked past them all and as I passed they held out their cards but there was no one with a board with 'Andrew Sadler' written on it as had been arranged. Everybody held up their boards as I walked by and eventually we gave up and went to the coffee shop, up some stairs.

The coffee shop was decidedly scruffy, even unclean. We ordered an Americano and a Cappuccino coffee for 340 rupees. There was no extra milk to add to the Americano. It was at this stage that Eric discovered that the fellow on the Dialog counter had thrown away his 02 sim card. He rushed back to the counter to see if he could retrieve it and fortunately he could.

Meanwhile I had gone back to the paging area but still there was nobody carrying a sign with my name on. It was now 7:00 a.m., more than two hours after our arrival time so we gave up and assumed that our pre-booked and pre-paid car was not coming.

I walked on my own outside the terminal to see if there should be anybody waiting there. There were whole crowds of people waiting around. It appeared to be that to get into the arrivals hall you had to pay for a ticket and if you were there to meet somebody and wanted to hold a paging board that too would cost 100 rupees. I returned into the arrivals hall and had to go through security and show my passport to get back in. I went to one of the two counters where taxis were being arranged. At the first one I was quoted 2,800 rupees for the ride to the Renuka Hotel. I went away and I was approached by a fellow on his own, who offered me a ride for 3,500 rupees so I decided to return to the first counter. I was then approached by a gentleman from the Sri Lanka Airport Drivers Association. He had a counter there as well and took me to it. He quoted me 2,600 rupees for the ride but told me I would have to pay a further 300 rupees for the road toll into Colombo. We decided to accept this. A form was filled in and we were taken outside to a car.

Meanwhile we had been asked if we needed a driver, to drive us around Sri Lanka, at any time during our visit. As we had previously arranged with the company who were supposed to be collecting us that we would want this service, I decided to ask the fellow his telephone number to get back in touch with him, as our arrangement previously made was unreliable. He took us to a car, our cases were loaded into the back and I noticed the driver giving the chap from the Drivers Association his commission, in cash. I light-heartedly asked the fellow what the etiquette was with regard to a tip and he said if I liked him, I should give him a tip, maybe 10% and everybody laughed at this. We set off from Bandaranaike Airport to Colombo.

Our driver was called Ishan he was our first real local contact and I was anxious to find out what his opinion was about the previous President Mahinda Rajapaksa. Rajapaksa was the President responsible for winning the civil war against the separatist LTTE (Liberation Tigers of Tamil Eelam) known as the Tamil Tigers. The war had been waging since the early 1980s but was won by the government forces under Rajapaksa in 2009. The end had been particularly brutal with allegations that the

Tigers were merging with the local population in the north and using them as human shields. Most of the Tigers were killed along with many civilians. However Rajapaksa failed to win the election of 2015 and one of his former ministers Maithripala Sirisena became President. I had heard that his rule after the war was very autocratic but I thought that surely after ending the misery of the war so decisively he would be a national hero, certainly with the Singhalese population?

Ishan said that President Rajapaksa was good to finish the War but he had also done some bad things as well, such as imprisoning one of the Judges. He felt that generally the Sinhalese got on very well with the Tamil minority of the population but that there were certain people in the north of the country who wanted to create a separate country, Eelam. Since the end of the War there had been an improvement in the economy but this had proceeded only slowly because the government had run out of money.

As we were driving along I notice that the general state of the vehicles on the road was very much improved from the last time I was in the country 22 years ago. Ishan had a modern Honda car with tread on the tyres, airbags and seatbelts. I asked him if he worked as a driver for tours around the country and he said he did. I asked him what his price was and he quoted 50 USD per day which was inclusive up to 100km. All charges were included apart from the occasional road toll. I asked him if I could contact him should we require this service as we had provisionally booked this but that it appeared the company was unreliable.

Ishan told us that a previous client who he had driven called him her 'Kind Companion' and so he used this name to promote himself and gave me his business card. This is how Ishan was to become our 'Kind Companion'.

The road into Colombo initially is very clear, a modern dual carriageway. We had to pay 300 rupees for the toll. As we neared Colombo, the opposite became the case. The roads were very congested and every vehicle that had a space in front of it moved forward to get into it, or even sideways but not backwards. The result appeared to be chaos but on the positive side there was constant movement and eventually we arrived at the Renuka Hotel where I gave Ishan 3,000 rupees. He asked me if I wanted any change and I said no, so he had a 400 rupee tip, which is about £2.00. We had Ishan's card and said that if he was available we would like to hire him to drive us when we had met my friends in Colombo; we would probably want to leave Colombo the following Sunday for seven nights away and I would email or call him.

Ishan Lokuhewa
Tour Operator

Mobile : +94 777 524505
+94 718 662332
Email : kindcompanion.sl@gmail.com
Web : kindcompanion.yolasite.com
Facebook : www.facebook.com/kindcompanion

4. First Day in Colombo. Renuka Hotel, Tea at Galle Face and Dinner with Old Friends

At the Renuka Hotel (328, Galle Road, 40000 Colombo), the room which we had hoped would be available from 8:00 a.m. was not yet ready, which I sort of expected; it was explained that the hotel was full last night and we could wait in the lounge. I asked him if it was possible to have some coffee and was told that the dining room was open for breakfast in the adjacent building. We went in, Eric had eggs on toast which was freshly prepared for him and I ate Sri Lankan food from the buffet. There were several different curries, cool in temperature and not too spicy, with coffee.

We went back to the lounge area where one of the receptionists (all male) helped me on to the internet on my Hudl (tablet computer). The first email I sent was to the fellow I had paid 36 USD for the airport transfer that had not materialised asking for my money back. By the time I had answered a few more e-mails a room was ready for us. We booked in, found the room and had a sleep.

The Renuka is very central, modern and comfortable. We had a large room with twin beds and a large bathroom and shower with noisy air conditioning and a window overlooking the side street.

We slept for several hours but at 4:00 p.m. local time we got up and after a shower walked down the Galle Road for tea at the Galle Face Hotel. I had wanted to stay at the Galle Face, it is a large old colonial style hotel (with new parts) near the centre of Colombo next to the sea. However I could not see on the web sites how we could be sure of booking twin beds. I had had tea there 22 years before with Maralyn and the children.

Galle Face is not far along the Galle Road from the Renuka. On the walk we were approached by several three wheeler drivers who wanted to drive us, and there were several others who pulled up for us but they went when I said no thank you. However two were not going to be put off by refusal and one was intent on persuading us to go somewhere other than the Galle Face Hotel with him.

The Galle Face is very smart and Eric and I had tea on the same veranda where I had eaten 22 years ago; it cost 600 rupees +100 rupee tip. This time there are none of the horrible aggressive crows that used to swoop down to pinch any food they could from your plate.

We returned to the Renuka for another shower and Panduka rang to say that he would pick us up from the hotel at 7:30. He arrived at close to 8:00 p.m. in his top of the range BMW SUV and we drove to his home somewhere just outside Colombo but we passed no countryside on the way. He told me that driving was very difficult in and around Colombo so when he went to work at the hospital he took a taxi because he did not want to drive.

We met Panduka's wife and his three daughters who spent most of the evening upstairs. We talked of old times and his pattern of work. Each day he works as a surgeon in the hospital for six hours. He can choose to work from 8:00 – 2:00 p.m. or do two 3 hour shifts but if he should come home from lunch, he would soon have to return to go back so he does all his work in the morning and then comes home. In the late afternoon and evening he does private work and sees patients and operates on two afternoons and evenings each week. He also runs his coconut plantation near to Kandy which was owned by his father, a former Dental Surgeon who gifted the plantation to Panduka. He enjoys supervising the plantations.

He told us that much of his work at the hospital involved supervision of his many trainees. He takes them through operations and then takes a back seat. Also he felt that guiding them through making decisions is as important as operating and

I agree with him. Trainee surgeons are potentially very dangerous and I used to keep a very close eye on them.

After about three quarters of an hour, Sam and his wife Savi arrived, Panduka's daughters came down to see them. They were already well known to Sam as he used to be their Dental Surgeon. The daughters are fed in the kitchens and then we all sit down to dinner with Panduka's wife Charmala and Savi and explained how the salad was made with squeezed coconuts and chilli and salt and a delicious mild potato curry made with potatoes cooked in different grades of coconut milk with turmeric. One of the dishes was stringhoppers. There are two types of stringhoppers made with either white or red rice.

At dinner I tried to learn more about the politics and that their opinions appeared to coincide with that of our driver Ishan yesterday. President Rajapaksa was very good in that he definitively ended the war of which they all approved but since he had ruled in a dictatorial way and because he was the hero, everybody did as he bid with bad consequences and that was why he was eventually voted out. Panduka said that there had been a lot of spending on infrastructure projects such as roads, hotels and buildings and an additional airport which was not needed and was not able to earn the revenue to pay off the debts and interests for the loans which had been made by China.

Sam has a talent for painting, particularly birds and he told us that he has his own website and uses it to sell his paintings. Panduka produced four framed pictures that Sam had painted of birds in the 1970s which usually resided on his walls upstairs. Sam said his paintings are not so good now but I think he is being modest.

There was a two-way conversation during dinner as Sam and Charmala have much to talk about it as they are obviously friends and have not seen each other for a while. Sam said he had insufficient time for painting now because so much of their time is taken up with babysitting for the grandchildren.

Time was getting on and Eric pointed out that Panduka has to go to work in the morning and he confirmed that he had a busy day ahead.

Sam and Savi went out of their way to drive us to the Renuka Hotel and we arrived there just before midnight.

Remember the images at:

www.twoinlanka.co.uk

5. Day 2. The Fort - Pettah Market - The National Museum - and Dinner with Indranee

We woke fairly late at 9:00 a.m. having slept well and had breakfast, curry and rice for me and eggs for Eric.

We took our first ride in a three wheeler from the hotel to the Fort area. Panduka had recommended that we visit the Old Dutch Hospital which has been renovated and restored and there was a shopping mall, although I am not interested in shopping. We were driven by a chap called David. I'd asked him for the price which seemed reasonable, 300 rupees.

The Old Dutch Hospital is quite small and has been converted into several high-end restaurants and shops, so we stayed no longer than five minutes. We then crossed the road and walked a short distance to the Hilton Hotel, where I used to go to read the English newspapers. However it had all changed and the bar where I used to go no longer exists so we left.

A recommended place to go in Colombo according to the Lonely Planet guide is Pettah Market. So we walked across the road and pass the central railway station to the nearby streets which were lined with shops and stall holders selling everything from clothing to tools. The streets were full of pedestrians, cars, motorcycles, three wheelers and chaps with carts moving coconuts and all sorts. It is very hot and Eric was unimpressed, so we stopped at a bar and had our first Elephant Ginger Beer in Sri Lanka, before taking a three wheeler to the National Museum where we learned about the ancient history of the country before another three wheeler took us back to the Renuka Hotel.

At 7:30 p.m., we took another ride to Indranee's house. I had telephoned her in the morning and she said to come in the evening for dinner. What a palaver it was finding her house! The driver said he knew Ward Place but he took us to Horton Place. He was trying to be helpful and stopped several times to ask people and eventually I phoned Indranee who gave instructions which did not help because I didn't realise we were in the wrong street. Eventually the driver asked somebody else and we were directed to Ward Place and then he bid me call Indranee, so he could speak to her which he did and so we eventually arrived.

I couldn't remember Indranee's house from 22 years ago. Her daughter had married and is in Louisiana in the United States and had produced two grandchildren and her son was at home, he is an Engineer who works in the docks. He started there after Indranee's Husband Rohan retired as an Engineer in the docks 10 years ago. Rohan now lectures in engineering at the University. We met her son but he ate in the kitchen, he said he wished to eat quickly and leave as he was off to visit his fiancée that evening. They were due to be married soon.

Dinner was served by a servant preceded by drinks. Indranee had retired from the Cancer Hospital but still worked in private practice, every day except for Sunday. Private practice takes place in the afternoon and early evening so she now has mornings free. Patients were mostly from Sri Lanka but she also sees patients from the Maldives and from the Seychelles. Now she no longer worked in the government sector, she said she had more time to spend with her patients. She was on call for her patients but there were medical officers in the hospital who look after them. They are not trainees or surgeons and care for all specialities so should a surgical problem arise she would need to attend. If she goes away, such as to visit her daughter in the United States, then there are other surgeons who take the cases because the patients with cancer cannot wait. She only does cancer surgery, no other general surgery. Some general surgeons are not pleased to have specialist cancer surgeons as they compete and take cases they might otherwise have.

Indranee thought President Rajapaksa should have had another six years as President before he was voted out. She said they know now how to sort out wars in Sri Lanka and thinks the European

Union is mad for letting in the migrants who are potentially dangerous as they are all Muslims and include terrorists who are intent on world domination.

Towards the end of the dinner, there was thunder and torrential rainfall. There were three tortoises in the garden and they were disturbed by this and were wandering around slowly. The Dalmatian dog was unperturbed. Rohan and Indranee drove us back to the Renuka Hotel in their 4x4.

There was good news. The money I paid for the airport transfer that did not happen had been paid back into my account and I had received an email of profuse apologies for the mistake. Due to currency fluctuation I had got back a few pence more than I paid.

Remember the images at:

www.twoinlanka.co.uk

6. Day 3 Visit to the Cancer Hospital - Mount Lavinia Hotel - Dinner near Independence Square

We both got up early at 7:00 a.m. as we had a date to go to the Cancer Hospital at Maharagama. Also today we were due to leave the Renuka Hotel and go to the Mount Lavinia Hotel for three nights. I had figured it would be noisy and dusty at the Renuka because it was on the main Galle Road but it had in fact been quiet, clean, comfortable and conveniently located. I asked at the desk for a taxi to take us to Mount Lavinia Hotel and drop off our bags and then on to the cancer Hospital at Maharagama. A phone call was made and a taxi ordered for 8:30 a.m. for 1,500 rupees.

After breakfast of chicken curry and rice for me and eggs on toast for Eric, we packed. We were given a receipt for the payment that had been made by credit card and we waited for a taxi. On arrival of a car the porter put our bags into the back and after some discussion in Sinhalese the bags were removed and we were told he was going to Hikkaduwa. After a short while a further discussion and the bags were put back in the car and we set off along the coast road and after approximately a mile we stopped and our bags were transferred to another car with another driver who took us to Mount Lavinia. I confirmed that the price was 1,500 rupees and the driver said he was told it was 1,700 rupees.

We dropped off our bags at the Mount Lavinia and half an hour later arrived at the Cancer Hospital, now renamed the Apeksha Hospital. We were let in through the gate and I paid the driver 2,000 rupees and we made our way to Ward 11, which appeared to be largely unchanged over the intervening 22 years since I was last there.

As we walked in through the door, I could hear Panduka's voice. He was sitting at the top of the table at the end of the ward opposite a large group of smartly dressed young men, at least seven of them, who he introduced as Registrars and Senior

Registrars. We told them that I had been there all those years before and he talked of people from the United Kingdom who had visited the Hospital and that there hadn't been anyone there for a long time and I explained that Oral and Maxillofacial Surgeons were now dominant in head and neck cancer management in the UK and that there was now plenty of surgical material for the trainees and that it was difficult for anybody to take time out of their training to go overseas.

We then set off on the ward round which was carried out in the same vein as all those years ago when Dr Gabriel was in charge. There were differences from then but they were few. Panduka was now not a trainee but the senior surgeon and the number of the trainees was considerably more. They followed Panduka around on the ward and said very little. Panduka demonstrated the cases and talked about them. Patients 22 years ago were examined intra orally wearing rubber gloves that were re-washed. Now disposable single use gloves were worn and there are no dogs to be seen anywhere on the ward. The beds were still close together and Panduka told us that they have less head and neck cancer cases now as the Oral & Maxillofacial surgeons were operating on many of them.

We were shown some post-operative cases which had recurrence of their original tumours. The first case is a chap with a large tumour invading his mandible which needed resection. Panduka told me that they no longer do free flaps[1] as the surgery takes too long and they could not afford six hours of operating time for a single patient. When the mandible needed resection they put in a reconstruction plate only and usually it holds. However the second patient we saw on the ward round has had this done and it has failed and the plate was erupting into his mouth and there was cancer growing around it, so he needed further surgery. We saw at least two patients who have buccal

---

[1] *Free flaps: free tissue transfer used in reconstruction after cancer surgery, a piece of tissue from another part of the body is sewed into place and artery and vein are attached using a microscope to suture.*

squamous carcinoma from chewing pann, the same number I saw in 20 years in the UK. There were a few patients with prostate cancer and several with soft tissue sarcomas and osteogenic sarcoma.

Only a little time was spent with each patient and there was very little explanation or discussions with the patients themselves, something that I thought would have changed with the new generation of surgeons. As before, the nurses were dressed in traditional nurse's uniforms with starched white aprons, all spotlessly clean without a stain or mark to be seen on any of them.

At the end of the ward there were two photographs on the wall in glass frames. One of the late great Dr Gabriel, another is a group photograph with him sitting in the centre and at the end, a young David Patton, a British Surgeon I know. The photos were quite faded with time and the one with David on must be well over 25 years old, as David is even older than me.

We then set off for the female ward upstairs where Panduka has only half of the beds allocated to him, so this part of the ward round is even quicker. There were some patients with mouth cancer, one with a basal cell carcinoma at the inner canthus of the eye, and one who had had a hindquarter amputation for a soft tissue sarcoma and had suffered a recurrence. There was another who was to have a leg amputation for an osteogenic sarcoma the following day.

After the ward round Panduka took us to see the operating theatre which was in the same place as before but was now an operating theatre suite all air-conditioned, whereas previously only the main theatre was air-conditioned. He told us that the air-conditioning failed several times a day but that there is an engineer on-site who soon got it going again. He introduced me to one of the senior nurses who was the only one who was employed when I was there. We did not recognise each other and I pointed out that when I was in the operating theatre, the nurses all wore full face masks.

I had remarked on the absence of dogs in and around the hospital compared to previously but as we pass along the corridor towards the operating theatre there is a particularly nice looking animal lying in the corridor outside the operating theatre scratching its itching belly with its teeth. We all laughed. Panduka referred to them as stray dogs which they probably are but I had read that a good number of them are simply free range and are owned or attached to some human being who feeds them and looks after them but they wander where they will. I remember Whips Cross Hospital and surrounds, many years ago, where there were many feral cats.

There was much construction work going on at the hospital and we walked through part of the construction site to the new outpatient building, where there was a woman having a colonoscopy in the endoscopy room. We waited in the adjacent office. There was a large new building being constructed which is going to house the surgical service. The old building which is now the home of the theatre and surgical wards are to be demolished.

We returned to Ward 11 to retrieve our bags and Panduka sent a fellow off to find a taxi for us. We waited outside the door and after a few minutes a three wheeler arrived and we told the driver we want to go to the Mount Lavinia Hotel but he turned his nose up to that and didn't want to take us, no explanation was given. We wandered through the main gate and approach another but he did not want to take us either and gesticulated to another driver. We crossed the road and we have found a deal. He asked us how many rupees we would pay. I asked him how much he wanted. He replied 700 rupees. I gave him 1,000 (no change).

We arrived at the Mount Lavinia Hotel and checked in. Our room was not ready yet, it was only just 1:00 p.m., so we took a seat in the lobby bar and drank Elephant Ginger Beer.

After about half an hour our room was ready and a very nice porter chap in a white uniform took us to it and insisted on taking our cases to Room 504 and on the way he told us some of the history of the hotel, which was the British Governor's residence and was the scene for the hospital in 'The Bridge on the River Kwai', which was filmed in Sri Lanka. We had an excellent twin bedded room and it was superior to the room at the Renuka only in that it had a private balcony overlooking the sea.

Later we sat on the terrace overlooking the pool and had afternoon tea. Then we set off for a walk along Hotel Road just outside the gate. There were several three wheelers and a chap with an old van asked us if we wanted a taxi. There was a fellow outside the gem shop who offered for us to go inside but we declined. A little way further on, we were joined by a man who engaged us in conversation and walked alongside me. He told me about the Buddhist temple nearby and asked me if I liked cricket and I said no it is too boring. Do I like rugby? No it is too dangerous. We walked on. I was getting nervous that he was about to touch me for some money but he was simply being friendly. He indicated his house and went off to it.

On the way back we saw the taxi man again and asked him for the price for a ride that evening to meet Panduka at Independent Square. He quoted us 1,500 rupees and we made a deal and arrange to meet him outside the hotel gate at 7:00 p.m.

In the evening, we arrived at the Senanayake Statue at Independent Square and took some photographs while we waited for Panduka and Charmala who had called to say that they will be 15 minutes late. They arrived 15 minutes later and after a short walk we took a seat outside a restaurant and ordered drinks. Panduka wanted me to have some beer but I asked for Elephant Ginger Beer but the waiter returned to say they haven't got any left, so I ordered Lion Lager but they didn't have that either, so I settled for a large bottle of Carlsberg which, when not yet finished, Panduka ordered another which we had with a pizza. After a bottle and a half of this Carlsberg I felt rather merry.

Perhaps it was stronger than I am used to or my recent decrease in drinking was taking some beneficial effect.

Panduka told us that there is plenty of work in the private sector. Treatment is quicker than in the government hospital and often after consultations, patients can be operated on the following day or soon after. In the government hospitals all treatment is free, as is all healthcare, but most patients will wait a couple of weeks for surgery or possibly a month if it is going to be a major operation that will take a lot of theatre time. He felt therefore that in the private system he was able to provide a better standard of care and I was inquisitive to know what sort of costs are involved but Panduka only said that the cost is beyond most people in the country to have private treatment (as indeed it is in the UK), but that they have now introduced insurance schemes.

Panduka and Charmala's eldest daughter intends to study to become a lawyer but there is a possibility of her studying medicine. She was doing London based A levels, as they give a wider curriculum, whereas the Sri Lankan Board ones are more restrictive and focused upon the intended courses at University so that a decision as to which career to follow has to be made at too early an age. If she wished to study law then this would be best accomplished in a Sri Lankan University but Medicine would be difficult as she was doing the wrong A levels.

They asked me about entrance to medical school in the United Kingdom. I told them that I was involved as an assessor for medical and dental schools entrance at Queen Mary University but they have a separate system for overseas entrants and that overseas fees would be enormous. I said that I believed that they kept a number of places free for overseas entrants but I didn't believe that any particular medical school had a reputation as being superior or inferior to any other but that living expenses would be higher in London. I suggested that they look at the websites of the universities that have medical schools which were all in the major cities and download the prospectus or e-mail to ask about admission requirements.

I said that now that the war was over surely less people would be leaving Sri Lanka to work overseas. I could see that there had been a lot of bright talent leaving the country. They replied that this was more than the war. Working conditions for professionals in Sri Lanka was not as good as in some other countries and they admired the fact that in the United Kingdom, people were generally very honest.

Panduka drove us back to the Mount Lavinia Hotel in his large BMW SUV. There were many police about. They had flagged down a number of vehicles including a car just in front of us on the Galle Road. I asked what they were up to. Panduka said that they were very low paid and needed to make an income and that if stopped you had to give them a tip to get away.

Sam had phoned in the morning to confirm that we should be at the golf club for dinner on Friday at 8:00 p.m. He had called Sandiya Abeyrathna to tell her that I was visiting the country. Sandiya had spent a year working with us in Lincoln, having been introduced by Dr Gabriel. She is now an Oral & Maxillofacial Surgeon in Kandy and intended to invite us to see her hospital when we were there

7. Day 4 Relaxation at Mount Lavinia -. A Walk on the Beach

We got up early at the Mount Lavinia Hotel and had fruit for breakfast. We spent most of the day sitting in the shade of the veranda writing and reading. In the late afternoon, we went for a walk along the beach as far as the Galle Road. We had to cross the railway line to get there and back.

The Mount Lavinia Hotel was originally built as the residence of the British Governor of Ceylon (as it then was). It was named Lavinia after his mistress (wife back in England). The hotel had its own railway station which is now the Mount Lavinia station. People visiting the beach get off the train and walk back along the track to the beach, it is not possible to get access to the beach without crossing the line. The trains do move slowly and make a lot of noise so there is little chance of injury.

On the beach there were a few people sitting under sun shelter belonging to hotels and we were approached by a couple of touts who wanted us to go to the hotels for drinks. There's quite a large number of dogs and a lot of rubbish, it is quite scruffy. At the Galle Road there was an English couple with a camera making a video of the traffic to take back home. They didn't believe that their friends would otherwise believe the driving technique. They said that they had witnessed two accidents on their holiday so far. We walked back to the hotel, where we had some Elephant Ginger Beer. After a shower we had Lion Lager and then dinner accompanied by water and Elephant and then watched the 'turn' by the pool, a trio playing pop songs with a keyboard, guitar and drum machine, and went early to bed.

Sam phoned in the morning to confirm that we should be at the golf club for dinner on Friday at 8:00 p.m. Sandiya had phoned in the afternoon to say that Sam had told her I was coming to Kandy on the 14th and she would like to meet me.

8. Day 5 Upset Stomach after Buffet - Exploration of Old Haunts - A Train Ride and Dinner at the Golf Club

Today I had planned to go out in the morning but I had an upset stomach for a while. I blamed the previous night's otherwise excellent buffet because the symptoms started about three hours later. I didn't want to be too far from the toilet facilities so I decided to stay and read by the pool in the morning. However by midday Loperamide and the passage of time had cured my problem and I felt ready to venture out.

I wanted to go for a walk to Queens Road where I lodged with Mrs Kadirigama in 1994. Eric had indicated that he did not want to go out in the most aggressive midday heat but had changed his mind, so we set off in a three wheeler to Queens Road and its junction with Duplication Road. The area was really unrecognisable because of all the recent development but we walked along Queens Road and I found Mrs Kadirigama's house, which appeared nearly almost unchanged, I took some photographs.

Eric got into conversation with a fellow at an adjacent building across the road who was telling him that this was the Queen's house. He asked him which Queen. He said Queen Elizabeth, it turned out that it was the British Council. We walked along Duplication Road. There were new buildings everywhere and no evidence of the Elite Hotel where I used to eat and I could not find the San Shi Palace Chinese either.

We walked along Duplication Road to Liberty Plaza which has been enlarged into the area of rough car park behind it and now there was now a multi-storey car park. The Plaza was now posher and I could not see any of the guards at the entrances which used to be there keeping undesirables out. I went to the stationery shop to buy two pens as mine had run out of ink.

We decided to try a new experience and get a train back to the Mount Lavinia Hotel from Kollupitiya Station. We walked towards the station but I couldn't get Google Maps to work on my tablet because it is just so complicated and we were a bit lost. A three wheeler turned up and touted Eric and he was persuaded, so soon we set off towards the station. Or so we thought. The driver was taking us in the opposite direction. He had sold himself as charging by the meter and therefore appears to be quite keen to take us on a ride all the way round Colombo to get us to a place which I believe is only a few hundred yards from where we started.

I then picked up our location on Google Maps and we were clearly going in the wrong direction and I got bad tempered. I told him he was going the wrong way and remonstrated with him but he told me that the roads are all one way. He then wanted us to go to some shopping area and I told him we are were not interested, we wanted to go to the station. He was also a pimp and he was offering us girls. However we did get back to the station. He then insisted that we tell him where we wanted to go because he wanted to take us and so I told him to piss off. We went into the station and we bought two tickets to Mount Lavinia which is three stops on the line, which cost us 20 rupees, 10 rupees each, which is five pence.

We waited on the very scruffy station for about 20 minutes. One train passed and we got the second train. It was reasonably crowded but nowhere near like the Central line in London at rush hour; we stood all the way to Mount Lavinia. The railway carriage was very scruffy, the doors were open to let in the air and there were cooling fans on the roof of the carriage, in fact lots of them. As the train trundled along we passed a lot of slum dwellings on the beach. When we reached our station we got off and found our taxi driver who had now upped the price for the ride to the golf club this evening and he had thus irritated me. In the hotel we got a beer and a ginger beer and I got a quote from the concierge for a ride to the golf club. The quote is the same as the fellow we have already arranged for at the gate, so I decide to stick with him.

We had a shower and met our driver a bit early at 7:00 p.m. and we set off through the traffic to the golf club. Soon before arrival, we got a call from Sam letting us know to call him when we arrived at the golf club and he would come and get us signed in. We subsequently found out that it is his son-in-law who is the member and a keen golfer. Sam and Savi and two daughters. One is a doctor working in Accident and Emergency with Anaesthesia. She wasn't sure whether she was going to undertake specialist training in Anaesthesia or Accident and Emergency Medicine. The other daughter is an Architect and is married to an Architect.

Eventually Panduka and Charmala arrived and we had a lovely evening with a drink and a meal all paid for by Sam. It was past 11:00 when we left and the driver has been waiting much longer than we agreed with him, so I gave him 5,000 rupees (£20.00), which is more than the 3,700 rupees agreed for the two rides and wait. The journey back to Mount Lavinia was much quicker as there was little traffic.

I had arranged for Ishan to collect us at 10:00 the following day to take us to Sigiriya but he has called to say from the traffic point of view, getting to Sigiriya in time to climb the rock before the heat tomorrow, it would be better to leave much earlier, even 4:00 a.m. We compromised at 7:30 a.m.

Before going out, I had telephoned Tilak. He was in a car en route between Kandy and Colombo. He said he would telephone and see us on Monday at the University. He said he would call me on Sunday to arrange a suitable time. Sandiya had called him to sort out a suitable arrangement so we could see her as well in the Kandy government teaching Hospital which is in the middle of Kandy and is separate from the University but they also take medical students and possibly dental as well. I'm was not yet sure - all would be revealed on Monday.

9. Day 6 Sigiriya & Reacquaintance with Ishan our Kind Companion

The project for today was to visit Sigiriya Rock the archaeological site that may have been a Buddhist monastery or some kind of fortress. I had visited before on my own but never climbed the rock because it was infested with touts and 'guides' who wouldn't leave you alone as they were after you money and I decided at that time just to leave to get some peace. I figured that if I was accompanied by a Sri Lankan it would be much easier this time.

We got up early at about 6:15 a.m. and packed our cases before checking out and paying for our dinners and drinks before breakfast. The fellow on reception said that if our driver said he was coming at 7:30 he would come at 8:00 a.m. (Sri Lankan time, he smiled). However at 7:25 a.m. Ishan called to say he is was the gate and later informed us that he had actually been there since 6:30 a.m. to avoid the traffic.

We set off through Colombo and he told us it would be quicker to take the new airport highway and then a shortcut rather than take the direct route to Sigiriya along the main Trincomalee Road. The traffic was much less on Saturday than a week day.

Once we passed out of the bustle of Colombo, we got onto the smooth new motorway which has been built out to the airport and stopped for the toll where Ishan asked us for the appropriate 300 rupees. Eventually, we turned off to more minor roads, taking a shortcut to the main Colombo to Trincomalee Road. Some of Ishan's relatives come from Trincomalee and he travels there twice a year.

Ishan mentions his boss. On questioning he tells me that he is not self-employed but works for a boss who is a family friend from the same village. He leases the car on a five year lease of 68,000 rupees and takes the fee we will pay and reimburses Ishan for all the expenses he has incurred, (fuel etc.) and gives Ishan

15%. Ishan will also earn commission from places he takes us to but he will only take us to what is best or least expensive places because the tourist industry depends on everybody getting a good deal and honesty and besides he is a Jehovah's Witness and must therefore be honest.

It appears that Ishan's driving is good but he likes to get from behind the lorries, many of which are belching out vast quantities of black smoke and at one stage I tried to point out that we are not in a hurry but too subtly, so later I asked him to slow down as we are not used to such speed and he does so. Of course it was not the actual speed I was concerned about but the speed we were travelling at the prevailing road conditions which we are not used to.

After several hours we reached Dambulla and a short while later we arrived at the drop-off point for the foreigner tourist car park at Sigiriya.

Ishan showed us where the ticket office is and said that he has to take the car to another car park and would hurry back. I said there was no hurry. We went to the ticket office and paid the 60 USD for our entrance and then Ishan arrived and paid his 1 USD Eric asked him if we should reimburse him, he said it was okay.

The place is very much improved since my previous visit. It is not possible for touts and self-appointed guides to tout their services and there are notices up to say that all guides must be registered and licensed. We walked from the car park towards the rock though the water gardens and eventually among the boulders at the bottom of the rock, it was very hot. In the gardens there are foundations of the ruined buildings and some stray dogs and some monkeys playing.

We started the ascent of steps up the rock. Ishan said he would come to the top of the rock with us but I said we were not certain we were going all the way up. When we had ascended the steps to the bottom of the metal staircase, Eric decided he would not go further (sensible) and I said to Ishan that he did not need to come with me. He said he had been at 40+ times with guests, so he went back with Eric.

I ascended the stairs as far as the cave in the side of the rock where the famous painted frescoes were. I decided that this narrow staircase up the side of the sheer face of rock was not for me and if possible I would go down at that stage. The frescos were very well preserved and I wondered if they had been touched up in modern times. There were four fellows sitting by them and I think their function was to stop people taking photographs, I assumed this because flash light would deteriorate them.

The route ahead from the frescoes was stone steps which would not induce any vertigo, so I decided to continue. I passed the 'mirror wall' with the ancient graffiti and soon reached a flat area with a first aid station and trees where you could sit in the shade. On approach I thought that this was the top but it is not.

After a short rest and a drink of water the route to the top is via some more metal stairs starting between the paws of the ancient lion statue. The metal stairs are held into the rock with concrete and it didn't appear to be at all unstable and less likely to induce vertigo. I waited until it was relatively clear of climbers so that I could ascend without interruption by dawdlers or children and set off.

The top of Sigiriya Rock was well worth the climb. There are multiple ruins of the bottom of walls of ancient buildings and a tank which looked like a swimming pool but was actually an ancient water storage facility. The view from the top is tremendous. I could now clearly see the Hill Country where we are to go tomorrow which from this vantage looks like mountains rather than hills. After a wander around taking many photographs, I descended.

My trip up had been facilitated in comfort by my fold up umbrella which has been most convenient for shading my head from the searing heat of the sun and for shielding the lens of the camera. On my way down a Japanese fellow said I am 'a very wise tourist'. I think an ascent in the early morning would be much more comfortable in terms of the heat but I wonder if there would have been greater crowds moving more slowly up these narrow staircases, which would cause me to be more vertiginous.

At the bottom I was guided by notices to the foreigner car park past several souvenir shops, many of them selling wood carvings as well as drinks and other paraphernalia. Eric and Ishan were waiting with the car and we drove a short distance to the Fresco Water Villa where Ishan said he has taken some guests before. On the way I saw our first elephant, bathing in a river at the side of the road. Ishan said there was another hotel that has rooms but I say this looks perfectly okay, it is 160 USD for half-board for one room for one night. Ishan's accommodation food is included and he would probably get a commission for taking us there.

No sooner were we in our room then he phoned to say a colleague had phoned to say we were paying too much but I said we should stay as the hotel is nice and we didn't want to move. There was a swimming pool outside our room and Wi-Fi in the restaurant and bar area. We went and had a ginger beer and a Lion Lager. They had Lion Ginger Beer not Elephant but it looked just as good but smaller bottles. Later I went for a sleep and sometime after I was woken by rowdy middle-aged swimmers in the pool. Eric thinks they are Ukrainian.

Dinner was from 7:30p.m. It was a buffet. I stayed in the restaurant area for a long while after eating, trying to download a Google Map, sending e-mails and writing my diary.

10. Day 7 Sigiriya to Kandy and a visit to the Queens Hotel

We woke up at 7:30 a.m. and it was so cool. We had had the ceiling fan on all night but not the air-conditioning. I opened the door to the veranda, there were a couple of fellows hoovering out the swimming pool, they grinned and waved at me. A little later I could see the restaurant was in business serving breakfasts to the tour groups who were up earlier than us. We had omelettes for breakfast, toast and coffee. During the trip I was eating breakfast because we were doing without lunch; Eric does not normally have lunch. I tried some banana oats with my omelette, only a very small portion. It was porridge, very sweet with slices of banana in it. I figured I could easily make this at home without the sugar.

We paid the bill for dinner, bed and breakfast, 160 USD, and the drinks extras in rupees. Ishan went to settle his bill; it appeared that he got his overnight accommodation without charge but had to pay 500 rupees for his meals. I presumed this comes out of the expenses from his boss as we have not been asked to settle this.

We set off towards Kandy. I confirmed with Ishan that he was being paid 15% of a fee as it seemed so little to Eric and me and he explained that while car and driver deals are being sold at 50 USD per day, they have to ask the same or will get no work.

The car was moving more slowly and I remarked on this and said we were pleased. In fact during the whole journey there was only one occasion when he overtook the vehicle in front blind on a bend. However Eric was insisting on sitting in the back again as it was more comfortable not being able to see the road ahead.

We drove for about 3½ - 4 hours. All the main roads pass through the centre of towns and villages and there is development and activity alongside all the roads. I was concerned about the welfare of the dogs. We passed one lying not dangerously close to the road asleep but actually on it. Ishan said there are some stray dogs around where he lives and his wife puts out leftover food for them so that they are not always malnourished.

Ishan said that he has contacted a friend in tourism who told him of two or three hotels with vacant rooms in Kandy which were recommended. There were not many vacancies because of the time of year; he said we could look at them and if not satisfied try another. When we got to Kandy he took us to a small hotel on the outskirts of the town which was difficult to find. On arrival we were given a glass of mango juice; however the room we were offered had only one double bed which was not acceptable and the alternative room we were shown downstairs which had two beds was scruffy with unhygienic looking mattresses and leaves all over the floor from the open window. We were told that it had not been made up as the occupants had not checked out but I doubted that it was occupied with no bedding at all and leaves on the floor so we decided that we were going to go somewhere else. Ishan said that he was told that there were twin beds.

Our next stop was the 'Peak Residence' close to the centre of Kandy; up a steep hill with several terraces with lovely views over the city and a clean room with two double beds for 60 USD, including breakfast.

After we settled in we had ginger beers in the lobby and then relaxed in the midday heat and then slept for a couple of hours. Later at about 5:30 p.m. and after a shower we walked down the hill and had more ginger beer and lager in that bar of the Queens Hotel where I had been 22 years ago. On my last visit I had been to Kandy for a Rugby game between the Royal School and Trinity College with some of their alumni. One of the schools had made the Queens Hotel their base for the week end and we spent several hours there drinking Lion Lager after the game. When I returned with the family a month or so later I had wanted us to stay at this lovely old building in the middle of the town but they did not have a room for us so we stayed elsewhere but we were able to use the hotel facilities including the swimming pool for payment. We had spent the large part of a day by the pool with our children Geoff and Kat swimming and we had had dinner there. I had wanted to stay there again this time but again it was full up. We went to the hotel and as with most other places it is much improved from how I remembered it. The hotel lobby is larger and smarter and the restaurant and bar are very smart. We had a drink in the bar and I took some photographs of the swimming pool where the children had played those years before.

We left the Queens and walked a little way down the street and had dinner in the White House which was not a success, although it was only 1,400 rupees for two. It seemed that much of the menu was not available and when we asked for an alternative it was not ordered from the kitchen so Eric ended up just having fried rice. There were a lot of beggars in the street in Kandy which there were not in Colombo, they including a lady outside the supermarket with three children sleeping on the pavement.

We got a three wheeler back up the hill to the hotel for 300 rupees. After we paid him Eric gave him 50 rupees tip. He laughed and said it must be the English way. We sat on the veranda in the cool breeze and Eric drank a beer and I had a coke. Later on we went downstairs to explore the restaurant in the hotel. Ishan was in there eating with some of the other drivers.

The hotel is beautifully situated with a balcony at the end of our corridor overlooking much of the town and the sports ground where I watched the rugby game in 1994. There seemed to be a lot of children there most of the time formed into patterns one of them spelling: '2016'.

11. Day 8 Teaching Hospital Kandy, Eric's Injury, Peradeniya University & Botanical Gardens

We awoke early; the early mornings are light long before it gets hot. Out of the window of our room we could see a lady in the adjacent house cooking breakfast in the kitchen and from the balcony at the end of the corridor there was sporting activity involving children on the sports field below. We had arranged to see Tilak at the Faculty of Dental Sciences. He had told us that we would have lunch with Sandiya later. Sandiya had telephoned to say that we should come to the teaching hospital at 9:00 a.m. Breakfast was served in the dining room downstairs (the hotel is on the side of a steep hill) and we ate freshly cooked omelettes. At every hotel there is a fellow in the dining area cooking omelettes on a gas stove with thick frying pans.

After breakfast we waited outside for Ishan and he was late, but not too much; he explained that there is one bathroom for four drivers in the accommodation. He dropped us inside the gate of the government teaching hospital which is actually very close by. I was now able to follow the journey on my tablet using Google Maps. I think Ishan took a wrong turning but could not explain my concern as he was in conversation one of his mobile phone for most of the journey. Inside the gate we called Sandiya as instructed and she told us to find the orthopaedic outpatient department, walk through the gate and she would send someone to meet us outside the surgical intensive care unit.

We easily found our destination as unlike NHS Hospitals the buildings are clearly labelled, in three languages (as nearly all signs in Sri Lankan are) Sinhalese, Tamil and English. After a few minutes a smartly dressed young man arrived to take us to see 'Madam' in the operating theatre. We went upstairs with him where he asked us to wait in the small, neat surgeons' room. While we waited an anaesthetist arrived and we chatted; he had spent some time training in one of the hospitals in London. Soon Sandiya arrived in theatre blues.

Sandiya had three patients to operate on that morning: two maxillary [mid-face] fractures from road accidents and a cancer case which had been cancelled as there was no intensive care bed available. Sandiya then took us on a tour of some of the patients on the wards. She has a ward allocated to her with the Plastic Surgeons next door; we met one of the Plastic Surgeons and saw several patients. There was a child Sandiya had repaired a cleft palette for (the lip having previously been repaired) and a couple of patients with carcinomas of the cheek as a result of pann chewing. They do not have any skin cancer cases; their skin is dark, Sandiya explains.

Sandiya is the only Oral & Maxillofacial Consultant but she has a good number of juniors in her department. She is always on call, but frequently the trauma cases are first admitted under the care of Neurosurgeons as they have head injuries and when she is away the juniors deal with most things but otherwise General Surgeons will take the cases and look after them for her. One day a week the academic department at Peradeniya University takes the trauma cases and she is not on call.

We then went to her Outpatient Department where there was work going on and a large number of nurses. Her consulting room is partitioned from the other dental chairs by a curtain and there are seats for observers of the consultations.

On leaving Eric banged his head on a piece of equipment near the door and dislodged some skin. He was clearly not the first to suffer this injury as the sharp edge had been covered with sticking plaster. We returned for him to have a dressing placed by one of the nurses. He sat in the dental chair for this, the first time he has sat in one for 16 years. Then we went to the doctors' lounge where we were given an apple drink and we then bid farewell to Sandiya and called Ishan to take us to the Faculty of Dental Sciences at Peradeniya for 11:00 a.m. to meet Tilak.

Ishan drove us to Peradeniya, only a few miles away. The traffic was very bad and we were moving slowly along the road when we noticed the Faculty of Dental Sciences on the side so we stopped and he dropped us off. There was a fellow at the gate of the car park who wanted to know where we were going and was totally confused when we said that we had come to see Professor Tilak. Eventually we realised we were better going into an alternative entrance. We introduced ourselves to another fellow at the main door and he took us along the corridor to Tilak's office where he was sitting at a grand chair and we sat on some sofas while he finished his conversation on the telephone.

There are two buildings for the Dental School, both modern. One is the pre-clinical and administrative building and the other is the dental teaching hospital. Tilak showed us around and took us to the teaching laboratory and showed us the anatomy dissection room with human cadavers stretched out on a stainless steel trolleys awaiting dissection. The medical and dental students in the UK no longer do human dissection but this dissecting room was just as it was when I went to Medical School 36 years ago and Dental School 46 years ago.

Tilak then took us over the road to the clinical building, a modern construction built around a small garden with open corridors. We saw several clinics with undergraduate students treating patients under supervision and visited the Oral and Maxillofacial Surgery ward and theatre. We saw the pathology preparation rooms and teaching laboratories. The surgeons were removing a soft tissue sarcoma from a child and had requested frozen sections[1] to check that the tumour was cleared. Tilak's opinion was requested and so we went to the reporting room and examined the sections with two of his pathology Professors. The tumour had all been removed and later we saw the child being wheeled from the operating theatre.

[1] *frozen section: after the surgeon has removed the cancer specimens are taken from around and frozen and stained for examination by the pathologist to ensure no cancer cells remain before the wound is closed*

We popped our heads into the back of a lecture theatre where the dental students were hearing a lecture on Pharmacology. We met Tilak's wife who is a Professor of Periodontology. She was on the clinic supervising students and we met several of the dental consultants who were treating patients or supervising students. The Oral and Maxillofacial Surgeons have their own intensive care unit which we visited. They were waiting for a patient from the operating theatre who was having a major cancer resection and reconstruction with a bony free flap.

Tilak asked me if I was willing to give a lecture to the students tomorrow morning. This I was reluctant to do as I was now four years retired and besides all my lecture presentations are on my computer in England and we were leaving Kandy early the next morning. Tilak says he keeps all his presentations on Google Drive so that he can access them anywhere in the world at any time.

We then left for a nearby restaurant, the Royal Restaurant. It is only a few hundred yards away but it was hot so we went in the Dean's vehicle. The Dean of the Dental Faculty has his own car and driver supplied. There we met Sandiya.

At the restaurant we had delicious Sri Lankan food. We were not allowed to pay, the Sri Lankan way is to provide hospitality for guests. We asked about the etiquette concerning tipping and how much we should add on for our driver. They told us that it is not the same as the Indian way. I have never been to India but there you tip a small amount for everything. I noticed that Sandiya left 100 rupees for the waiter (although it was a buffet).

There we said goodbye to Sandiya and we went with Tilak a few hundred yards and he dropped us off at the entrance to the Peradeniya Botanical Gardens. We paid 2,200 rupees for us both to enter and we walked around. It was very hot and I noticed that facilities in terms of toilets etc. are much improved since 22 years ago. Apart from the enormous trees, we saw loads of monkeys and flying foxes in the trees and the footbridge over the

Mahaweli River which I walked over all those years before. There is a notice saying that only six people are allowed on the bridge at a time and although there was a fellow manning the entrance, there were well over six people on it at the time.

We stopped at the cafe where we ate all those years ago and had ginger beer, they were also serving lunch. There are additional catering buildings there and the cafe looks much modernised with improved plumbing. The botanical gardens are spectacular and we enjoyed walking around even though it was very hot and I don't have any knowledge or previous interest of the different species of tree. The gardens were used as the site of the British headquarters in the film 'The Bridge on the River Kwai' and were actually Mountbatten's Headquarters in the Second World War. We called Ishan who then collected us and took us back to the hotel.

In the evening, we walked a short distance down the hill to an open restaurant with views over the town where we ate a Sri Lankan vegetable biryani with ginger beer. On the way down we met a lone cow walking up the road; she didn't take any notice of us. On the way back we were followed by a dog who got friendly and jumped up and covered Eric's pristine trousers with mud.

12. Day 9 Tea Factory, Nuwara Eliya, the Hill Club and Grand Hotel

We had an early breakfast at the hotel, omelettes, and left for Nuwara Eliya. Ishan had arranged for us to stay at 'The White House'; it looked quite impressive on their web site.

We travelled more slowly now and we were not in a hurry; the traffic was dense for several miles out of Kandy. On the way I recognised the Kandy prison from my previous visit. Ishan said that it was closed now and due to be converted into some sort of museum.

Ishan gave us a history of how he started driving which was his hobby as well as his job. He started cycling and then progressed to motorbikes and as a child he cleaned cars for the fellow who he now works for and as his payment he was allowed to drive for 10 to 15 minutes before he was legally allowed to do so.

As we ascended the twisting roads into the Hill Country we did not notice the decrease in the outside temperature because of the air-conditioning but we did notice the lovely scenery and that the roads were neat, often with flowers alongside and the orderly rows of tea in the plantations with notices indicating their names. There was also a smattering of hotels and a good number of tourist buses on the road.

We stopped at a sort of lay-by at the side of the road where there were a few other tourists taking photographs of the scenery. We were immediately pounced on by two elderly ladies who wanted me to take photos of them holding flowers. I took a picture and retrieved my wallet from my trousers and gave 50 rupees. However this was not enough and the one who had received the note was pointing at the other lady which was, I assume, an indication that I should give her money as well. She was also pointing at my wallet which I took to be that there were still rupees in there which needed to be handed over. Another lady came and assumed a pose and I gave her 20 rupees, again not enough. An English fellow was there taking pictures. He said I could take his photo for 1,000 rupees.

We drove along the winding and relentlessly uphill road past the next tea plantations until we came to the 'Glenloch' plantation. There was a car park brimming with tourist buses and cars. After parking we were organised into parties where we were shown through the tea factory by a guide. We saw where the tea leaves were being dried, on a long conveyor belt with fans pumping warm air from below, and then being cut up by machines and sorted and eventually the final product which were bags of tea ready to be sold at auction. Different parts of the plant are used for different teas; black tea from the leaves, green tea from the stalks and finally white tea from the tips; this is the most expensive. The majority was black tea, Orange Pekoe, which we know as English Breakfast tea. There were notices up asking us not to give tips to the staff but if we want to leave a tip to place it in the tip box as we exited. I left 10 USD.

Then were then taken to a separate building where we were given seats and tea was brought for us to have a cup. All of this was entirely free but we had the opportunity to buy tea in the shop. I bought some mint flavoured green tea.

When we got to Nuwara Eliya I asked Ishan if we could stop at the Grand Hotel as I had stayed there before with Maralyn and the kids. I wanted to enquire if we could have dinner there; I went to the reception desk to ask. I recognised part of the hotel but it has been substantially upgraded since we were last there. I was told that they would be pleased to give us dinner. If we wished to eat in the main restaurant rather than in the Indian, Thai or Italian, it would be best after 9:00 p.m. as they were quite full with bookings. We were told we could arrive earlier and have a drink in the bar.

We arrived at the White House where we were to stay; it was away from the main part of the town past Gregory's Lake. The house looks nice from a distance but the car park was strewn with litter and there was an unpleasant musty smell inside and the stairs and hallways were untidy and not very clean. Our room was scruffy but at least we had a bed each and an en-suite shower room.

We decided to walk into Nuwara Eliya. I had previously been told about the Hill Club and read about the afternoon tea there which was discussed and recommended in Lonely Planet; we decided to see if we could blag our way in. The Hill Club was identified only by its location on a map; there are no signs outside. We asked a gardener at the gate if this was the Hill Club and he confirmed that it was and so we made our way up the drive through the immaculate gardens to the door where we asked if we could have tea.

The answer was 'of course' and then we were given a conducted tour by a chap in uniform. The premises seemed to be deserted at 2:30 p.m. Eventually we were seated at the end of the formal dining room in easy chairs and tea was brought and we were asked if we wanted high tea and so we ordered. We were told it would take half an hour as all was freshly prepared. There was a German couple sitting near us and later a young English couple at some distance who were asking for the prices and doing currency conversions on their phones. Eventually a coach arrived and discharged a load of Japanese tourists who traipsed through the dining room to another room for tea. Eventually sandwiches, spring rolls and cake arrived which we ate with the tea and a bill was issued for the high tea and 100 rupees each for day membership; day membership was open to foreigners only. Eric paid the 5,000 rupees that it all came to and later Ishan told us that was enough to buy tea for a month.

We walked back to Gregory's Lake and there a three wheeler drew up alongside us and quoted us 200 rupees for a ride to the White House. However it soon became apparent that the driver didn't know where it was although he previously said he did. We, of course, did know and as he had gone much further than he thought he would have to we gave him 300 rupees. There did seem to be quite a number of people who say they know where somewhere is but actually don't.

At the hotel there was a water boiler high up in the wall of our shower room. There must have been something wrong with the tap because the water that issued forth was either cold or scalding hot and it was very difficult to get a comfortable temperature. After we had showers Ishan drove us back into town for dinner at the Grand Hotel. We found the bar which was crowded mostly with senior English ladies who were making up a group tour. We had beer and white wine and chatted for a long time. The bar was uncomfortably crowded and cold. There was a log fire smouldering in the fireplace but the window was wide open and cold air was blowing in. Eric went and mostly closed it but a bit later, one of the staff opened it wide again. There was a billiard room next to the bar where our son Geoff played with the resident player 22 years ago. At that time there was a sign up giving the price for the first tear of the cloth over the billiard table, there is still a notice to that effect. However there are now three billiard tables in the enlarged room rather than the previous one.

We were told on arrival that we could have dinner in the main dining room after 8:30 p.m. At the dining room we were told we must buy a ticket for the buffet from the adjacent cashier which we did for 6,600 rupees. We were shown a table in the restaurant and ordered fizzy water to drink and then we were invited to help ourselves from the magnificent buffet with a wide and varied choice of food. After soup I ate mostly Sri Lankan food but there was a nice Indian style biryani as well.

We were nearly finished when Ishan called to ask if we wanted a lift back and we arranged for him to come in 20 minutes to take us back to the White House.

13. Day 10 Ella in the Hill Country

We did not have a good night at the White House. It was cold with no availability of heating. The beds had an under sheet and just a blanket over it with no other sheet. Eric was cold but I was prepared with a T-shirt to wear as well as pyjamas and a woolly jumper. Sleep was delayed by barking dogs which went on for ages. In the morning there was heavy traffic noise and when we woke and got up and mastered the shower everyone else had eaten and left; but they were very obliging and made some breakfast for us. We were offered omelettes but we only wanted coffee and fruit. They also brought some toast; I particularly appreciated the papaya fruit.

We didn't want to stay another night. Apart from the shower and the barking dogs the skies were overcast with rain clouds, it was misty and cold and besides we had seen the best of Nuwara Eliya. Ishan had anticipated this and told us there were rooms available at the Alta Vista Hotel in Ella.

We packed up and paid 60 USD and left. Ishan drove us into town and I changed 100 USD into 142,000 rupees. I went to the Bank of Ceylon and stood in one of two queues for the counter and was picked out by one of the staff who beckoned me to one of the seats at another counter. Why I was getting, what appeared to me to be, preferential treatment I was not sure.

Ishan told us he had had a chat with the proprietor of the White House and told him that the rooms were not up to standard for the tourist trade for foreigners. He told me that the gentleman had just taken over renting the White House from its owner and that he was an accomplished chef himself, previously working at accommodation at one of the tea plantations and he was trying to push the catering there for lunch and dinner. I must say that the dining room was very neatly and attractively set out but it could have done with some tender loving care elsewhere and the rubbish cleared out from around the house outside.

We left Nuwara Eliya and drove along the main road, following the same route that we must have passed 22 years before. I particularly recognised passing some botanical gardens where we had stopped in the lay-by opposite and the children fed some wild monkeys. Now there were stalls selling various goods at the same place and the whole area had been upgraded. The roads in particular were very much better. Ishan said that the previous President Rajapaksa was responsible for doing this but rather than praising him for the improvement in the infrastructure, rather he thinks this was all done so that he could get commission for the work. It was paid for he said by low interest loans provided by the Chinese government.

We arrived at Ella about lunchtime. The Alta Vista Hotel is up a steep driveway from the middle of the village. It is a modern hotel with rooms with balconies and a nice view over the village and the hills around about. We were pleased with the hotel and location and went for a walk around the village, which didn't take very long, and then for a beer and a ginger beer at Chill, which is a cafe recommended by the hotel. We were joined by Ishan after he confirmed that he would not be required to drive us again that day.

Ella is a lovely village in the Hill Country. It was warmer than Nuwara Eliya but still much cooler than where we were on the coast at Colombo. There appeared to a lot of western tourists with restaurants and guest houses to accommodate their needs. The village is surrounded by hills which makes the outlook attractive and interesting in all directions. A lot of the tourists appeared to be young people which I suspected was because the village is on the railway line.

It seemed very odd to us that the hotel where we were staying does meals including dinner but the man in charge recommended that we go to Chill in the middle of the village close to the end of the hotel drive. He said that they have a wider range of food and beers for us to drink that the hotel does not. Could you imagine a hotel at home which does catering suggesting that you would be better off eating elsewhere?

After we had had a drink we returned to the hotel and after a short sleep discovered that the hotel's deficiency was that our electricity plugs wouldn't fit into the three pin sockets in the walls and the adaptor they had supplied didn't work. We therefore had to take turns at one of their sockets in the lounge dining area to charge our various appliances.

Later we set off for the short walk to Chill for dinner. There is another cafe next to Chill which is run by the brother of the proprietor of Chill. We went down at about 6:15 p.m. and it was very busy but we found a table for two near the entrance and drank some Lion Lager and ate some delicious Sri Lankan food before returning to the hotel. Most of the clientele of the restaurant appeared to be tourists; all sorts of food was served there including Sri Lankan and Western. There was a fat Welsh bloke at the adjacent table tucking into a burger and chips like he needed even more calories to expand his already impressive girth.

14. Day 11. Ella and the Trains

This was probably the laziest day so far. We went to bed early the night before and I had the intention of walking up Little Adam's Peak. It is a prominent pointed hill about 1½ km from the village along the road and then a climb through the tea plantations to the peak itself with fine views over the countryside. From what I read, the walk through the tea plantation is as good as the summit which we could see from the window of the dining area of the hotel. Eric had decided not to go as he was a bit puffed coming up the steep drive to the hotel from the centre of the village. The perceived wisdom is to climb Adam's Peak early in the morning before mist descends and before it rains. I decided to go later but the weather was very changeable; the view of the peak may be clear and sunny but within half an hour it could become overcast and raining. In the end I didn't go. We sat and read until lunchtime and then went to Chill for coffee and a fried vegetable snack.

The most exciting part of the day was our trip to the railway station, which was a short walk away, to see the arrival of the goods train. The station has won prizes for being the best kept station in Sri Lanka and it was mostly neat and tidy, although the car park was strewn with litter. We could tell that something exciting was about to happen because taxis and three wheelers were arriving to catch people who might be leaving the train. There was a Buddha statue opposite the station and there were five dogs hanging around. One of the dogs was attempting to mount one of the bitches.

There was a map of the rail system displayed at the station and a timetable and a list of prices. I think the train is probably a nice way to see the Hill Country; I think I might go again and travel by train. I think you can book trains in advance with reserved seats in some of the carriages. There were only a few trains each day coming to Ella.

The train arrived with much noise. There was a diesel engine drawing five oil tanks with one second-class passenger coach behind and a passenger 'observation coach' at the end. The passenger coach was as crowded as the Central Line in the London rush hour and it appeared that many dozens of passengers got off. They appeared to be mostly young backpackers. Only a few passengers got on the train as Ella is the penultimate station on the line. The three wheelers and taxi drivers were trying to persuade people that they needed a taxi but Ella is very small and all the guesthouses are an easy walk.

We spent the rest of the day reading and went for dinner at Chill where we had Lion Lager with the food. I tried some buffalo curd for the first time on this visit to Sri Lanka. It looks like ice cream and was sweet and delicious.

It had been a pleasant restful day warm and sunny most of the time with intermittent showers, and overcast for part of the time but with the clouds moving on quickly.

15. Day 12. Hill Country Ella to Unawatuna Beach Resort

We woke up early with the intention of leaving at 8:30 a.m. It was cool, bright and sunny and Little Adam's Peak was clearly visible and this would have been a good time to go. Ishan was in the dining room with other drivers. After we had breakfast we were ready to go but it appeared that Ishan had not had his, so the start was delayed until 9:00 a.m.

I particularly wanted to visit Galle and if possible have dinner at the New Orient Hotel. When I was here before the proprietor used to stay at the swimming club in Colombo, which I had joined as a temporary member, and we used to have a drink together. He was killed in a road accident a few days after I left. Ishan said that Galle hotels are mostly fully booked and are very expensive so suggested we stay at Unawatuna which is a beach resort only a few miles away where there are more and cheaper hotels. I was quite happy with that, one of the authors of the books I read had stayed there for similar reasons.

We set off south. There were quite a few road works going on where they were repairing after landslides a year or so ago. However most of the roads were considerably improved since we were here before; most of them are in quite good condition.

We stopped at Rowanna Falls, an enormous waterfall at the side of the road. Ishan pulled the car up into a little lay-by. There were a number of tourists who had stopped and who like us were taking photographs and some of them were climbing onto the rocks. There were several people selling things; one was a fellow who was boiling corn in a pot over a fire. We only stopped for a few minutes but just as we were about to go, the car was approached by a chap selling parking tickets. Ishan brushed him off. He said he had no legal authority to do so; he was just a fellow who had some tickets printed and was attempting to con people out of a few rupees.

Later on we passed some enormous lakes. These are artificial reservoirs called tanks which retain water used for irrigation of the paddy fields. We were now in the area from which former President Rajapaksa came. Ishan explained that he was the first President from this part of the country and although he was no longer in post he was still involved with the government; there are quite a number of photographs of him around and things bearing his name. These include an international capacity airport, which is largely not used, and a convention centre which Ishan explained was little used because it is too far from Colombo and there are no five-star hotels nearby.

We drove along some of the new dual carriageway road close to the coast but mostly the more conventional highways passing through towns and villages with residences, commerce and activities all around. Amongst the places that we passed through was Marissa which is renowned as the best place to go to watch blue whales from 12km off the coast. There were several hoardings along the side of the road advertising whale watching trips. We also passed through Welligama which is the best place on the coast for surfing and where we stayed overnight many years previously.

Eventually we got to Unawatuna, which is a beach holiday resort. Ishan had made some enquiries on the telephone and had some potential places to stay arranged. We drove off the main road down very narrow side streets towards the beach. Ishan believed it would be best to stay near the beach. He called at one nice looking hotel but apparently there was some confusion as to whether we could or could not stay there; it depended on someone who was not there at the moment. The second place we called at had no room. There were others that Ishan had declared not suitable.

Soon we found a hotel which could take us; of course we had to have a hotel which had accommodation for Ishan as well. We were shown the room which had a small patio with a table and chair, a room with one double bed and an en-suite shower room. This seemed very suitable but we explained we are not so friendly that we are prepared to share a bed; however they did have another similar room in the adjacent building. I asked the owner how much for two rooms. The price was 40 USD for the room for bed and breakfast and he said for 70 USD we could have two rooms, so we took that deal.

After we had unpacked our suitcases, we decided to take a stroll along the lane, the other side of which are more shops and residences and cafes and the beach just behind them. It was very hot and we were only a short stroll from the Hot Rock restaurant where we took a seat at a table close to the bar. There were numerous tables with chairs under awnings on the beach and lots of people lying on the beach or swimming in the sea. We ordered some Lion Lagers.

There were a group of young people sitting at a large table adjacent to us. A young lady arrived from the sea wearing a bikini so small that if I was colour blind I would not know of its existence. She leant over the fellow closest to me to pick something up and he started slapping and fondling her arse about 2½ feet from my face. 'Stop, no more,' I exclaimed. 'I am an old man and this might give me heart trouble.' 'It will keep you young', the fellow replied. I told him that my wife would not want me back either excited or dead. They were a group who were on holiday from Siberia. The couple in the room next to me in the hotel were from Finland and those in the room next to Eric from Denmark. The next day we spoke to a young couple from the Ukraine. It appeared there were a large number of people here from Northern Europe who were escaping their winters.

After a couple of Lion Lagers we returned to the hotel for showers. There were nice covers on the beds but no sheets. We found the 'boy' who was in charge of our rooms and he brought and fitted mosquito nets to the beds but only one sheet. It appears you sleep on a sheet with nothing over you which turned out to work very well for me.

    Later we returned to the Hot Rock for dinner with Ishan. I drank ginger beer and had Sri Lankan curry and rice and afterwards we went early to bed. I awoke at 3:00 a.m. and turned the air-conditioning off. It was quite comfortable at night without it.

16. Day 13. Galle, the Dutch Fort and Back to Mount Lavinia

We got up fairly early and after a shower I went and knocked for Eric in his room, he had just got up. Ishan was waiting by the car.

Eric and I sat outside his room and the 'boy' came and asked us what we wanted for breakfast, omelettes perhaps? We confirmed omelettes would be fine and he brought us an omelette each, toast, coffee, marmalade, butter and a plate of fresh fruit each, bananas, watermelon and tangerines. Later the 'boy' came with a bill and I paid the 70 USD and I also paid Ishan his 400 USD fee and 100 USD gratuity.

We set off for Galle. I wanted to stop at the Dutch Fort area and have a walk around the walls. Ishan had driven us in through one of the two entrance gates in the wall and said he would drive us around the Fort area and park the car. He parked the car opposite the old New Oriental Hotel which is now called the Amangall. It now costs over 300 USD per night to stay there. We had already had breakfast so decided not to attempt any dining there. We walked around and took some photographs. The whole of the area is now very upmarket and smarter than I ever remember it.

I got into conversation with the owner of a gem shop that I walked past and he told me that the tsunami of 2004 wrecked much of Galle and as a result there had been a lot of development and reconstruction. However, the tsunami did not damage the inside of the Fort due to the high walls.

I decided to climb up the wall and get a view over the international cricket ground. A three wheeler driver was keen to take me on a three hour tour of the Fort but when I told him we were about to leave anyway he reduced the time and the price. There were two lots of photographers at work taking photographs for a wedding rehearsal. It was not the wedding that day, just a practice run.

Ishan asked us if we would like to see a wood carving factory. I wanted to bring a mask back home so we drove to a place not far away in Galle. We were greeted from the car by a fellow who was to be our guide and salesperson. There were a couple of chaps carving Buddhas from teak and he showed us how they made the natural colours for the masks from wood. He carved reddish coloured wood and added it to hot water to make the red, then metal dust to make dark brown and then lemon juice to make it yellow then calcium carbonate to make dark red again. We were then taken to a show room where we admired a coffee table which turned over to become a chess set. The price was quoted in rupees which I worked out on my calculator on my phone to be £2,500 including shipped to England. I bought a mask for 65 USD, and as I had shown interest in the chess set coffee table I was led back to it and asked what was my 'budget'. Clearly they were in for bargaining but I had to explain that I didn't have a 'budget'; the table was really lovely and beautifully crafted but I simply was not in the market for one. I'm sure such an object would cost much more in England but I suspected I had overpaid for the mask.

We drove back to Mount Lavinia along the new road that former President Rajapaksa commissioned and nearer Colombo we drove along the old Galle Road to Mount Lavinia. We passed rubber, tea, coconut and cinnamon plantations. Once we got to the built up areas again the traffic was moving at frightening speeds but we got there without injury or collision. While passing the rubber plantations Ishan told us that some of the Europeans he has driven do not realise that rubber comes from trees but rather think it is simply made in a factory. The cinnamon trees appear to be quite small. The cinnamon bark is harvested by cutting off the branches and then the bark is removed. The rest of the branches make very good firewood, particularly for barbecues, because when the wood burns it gives off that lovely cinnamon smell.

At the Mount Lavinia Hotel, we waited in the lobby for ages for a room to be ready. We had arrived an hour and a quarter before booking in time. There was a wedding party of bride and bridesmaids and what appeared to be five photographers at work, taking a vast number of images of them with remote lighting; the photography went on for well over half an hour. Apart from a well-dressed elderly couple, there didn't appear to be any other guests. Eventually I asked one of the photographers' assistants where they were but I didn't think he understood me. In the evening after having a shower we ate in the hotel at the buffet; it was Italian evening. Again there was a band playing on the terrace near the swimming pool and after we had finished eating in the indoor restaurant we moved to a table outside to have coffee and listen to the music.

17. Day 14. Another Day at Mount Lavinia

I woke up fairly early after a somewhat disturbed night with upset digestion. Twice we had eaten from the buffet at the Mount Lavinia Hotel and twice I had started with diarrhoea within three hours. It seemed odd that I had had no problems throughout the trip except after eating at the most expensive hotel we had stayed at. However the symptoms settled after three hours and two Loperamide tablets. Eric was not affected.

I was confident breakfast would be no problem as we were having omelettes, which were served everywhere we had been, and were cooked in front of you with the fillings added according to request. The toast you made yourself on a toasting machine, as at many hotels at home and the coffee was okay.

It was very hot but there was a cool breeze on the terrace so after breakfast, we found a spot in the shade opposite the swimming pool, where we spent most of the day reading and following the UK news on our tablets.

There was a small wooden platform in front of us where a fellow was unloading amplification equipment for the jazz band which would be playing to accompany Sunday brunch. It seemed that each day instead of cleaning the platform, someone comes and paints it with white paint. This morning he was painting the platform around the equipment that had already been put on it. The jazz band was excellent but we did not have any food.

There appeared to be more local people in the hotel. Perhaps it is because they were having a longer weekend because the following day was to be a full moon and Poya Day, which occurs every full moon and is a religious holidays for Buddhists. Later in the day a note came under the bedroom door to tell us that no alcohol would be served on Monday because it was Poya Day. Yesterday I had told Ishan that when I was working in the hospital, we did not operate on Poya Day because the fellow who swatted the flies in the operating theatre was a Buddhist and not allowed to kill anything then. I had assumed they were pulling my leg but Ishan told me that they must not set even a mouse trap on Poya Day.

In the late afternoon, after we had had a shower and the heat had reduced, we went for a walk down Hotel Road. We investigated the hotel seafood restaurant on the beach but decided against it because of the sand and mosquitoes. We decided to eat from the buffet but I had only soup and some chicken and potatoes that were cooked by a chef on the terrace in front of us with bananas to follow. Success, no adverse effects. I went to bed early.

18. Day 15. Home

We arose early just before the alarm which was set for 6:30 a.m. We showered and packed and then went to settle the bill for the dinners and drinks using dollars to deplete our foreign currency.

After breakfast, we cleared the room. Ishan was due at 8:00 a.m. but by 7:45 a.m. he was already there so we set off for the airport early. As it was Poya Day there was not much traffic around as most people were not at work, so he said that we could take the ordinary road and we would still be at the airport in time. I said we were happy to pay the 300 rupees toll for the express road and be at the airport very early. On the way to the airport, he told us about a carved tray that he was selling on behalf of a friend. The fellow who carves them has no legs and is very poor and it would help him if I were to buy one of the trays for 32 USD. He also quoted the rupee price. I handed over 310 rupees for the 300 rupees toll for the road but the toll fellow did not have 10 rupees change. We laughed.

At the airport Ishan showed us one of the trays which was in the boot of the car. It was small enough to fit in my hand luggage. So I paid him 30 USD and 500 rupees. We had managed the currency well and had only a couple of pounds worth of rupees left between us.

At the airport we had to show our passports to get into the terminal building, then we went through security, then the check-in desk, then more security, then immigration (even though we were going out). Then we waited in the departure area which was very smart with shops and restaurants and prices all in USD. I spent 5 USD on a blue elephant for Maralyn and deposited my last few rupees into a charity box before we left.

We arrived back at London Heathrow on time at just after 7.00 pm. England seemed very cold.

19. Appendix 1 Why you should not drive in Sri Lanka

I made some enquiries on-line about hiring a car. Although I had driven there myself 22 years ago I was a little put off by reports I had read which advised against. I contacted a car hire company in Colombo who provided some quotes but with them came this warning which I have reproduced below.

We decided to take advice and hire a car with driver which was not much more expensive. One of the deciding factors was that all the on-line car hire brokers I had dealt with in the past were quoting a 3000 euro deposit from my credit card. I anticipated that with all the bureaucracy I had witnessed in Sri Lanka before that in the event of an accident or dishonesty I might have hassle getting an insurer to refund the deposit.

'Self Drive Vehicles

Driving on Sri Lankan roads can be tricky. Although the country has a few expressways up to international standards, not all roads adhere to such standards. As such when one leaves the expressway or highway, the roads can be less marked with direction boards, road lines, etc.

There is also the fact that domesticated animals walk along the roads unattended.

When passing through villages, children can be playing on the roads, pavement hawkers and shoppers getting about their business on the roadside, busses arbitrarily stopping for passengers, motor bikes and tuk tuks wizzing in and out of traffic without following lane discipline. Talking about lane discipline, this is one of the most ignored facts about driving on the roads here.

Whilst veteran drivers will not be ruffled by these scenarios, a driver from a very disciplined environment can find it very distracting to drive here. Apart from the danger of not kowing what to do in a difficult situation and getting into trouble, one could also get into a minor scrape that will lead to legal proceedings and maybe best avoided if sorted out on the spot of the accident with the other party.

If sorting out on the spot, do not look for justice and fairness as more often than not there are arguments about who was wrong and this will not even have any logic to the claims leveled. So be prepared to pay your way out ad save time and hassle and get on with your journey.

If you are familiar about these facts about driving in Sri Lanka, you could then consider self drive as an option. Do not think of trying out driving here just to experience it since it is not a pleasant experience for someone not knowing how to handle it here.'

20. Appendix 2 Accounts

Currency paid in:	Pounds	US dollars	Rupees
Two air fares London to Colombo	1226.30		
ETA (visa) $35 each)	49.03		
DEET, Loperamide & sunscreen	33.50		
Two local SIM cards & credit			2600
Hotels Booked on-line (B&B)			
Renuka Colombo 2 nights	173.79		
Mount Lavinia 3 nights	399.94		
Mount Lavinia 2 nights	248.86		
Hotel Booked by Ishan			
Fresco Water Villia Sigiriya (half board)		160	
Peak Residence Kandy 2nights		120	
White house Nuwara Eliya		60	
Alta Vista Ella 2 nights		140	
Unawatuna 2 rooms		70	
Meals & Drinks		147	
Meals & Drinks			49946
Taxis & 3 wheelers			20980
Train fares			20
Admissions			
Colombo museum			1200
Sigiriya		60	
Botanical gardens Kandy			2200
Gratuities not included above			2650
Gratuities not included above		10	
Ishan fee for car & driving		400	
Ishan gratuity		100	
Total	2131.42	1267	79596

We changed sterling to dollars for $1.41 per £ and dollars to rupees for 141.5 rupees per $. Thus grand total was £3428.95 or £1714.47 each but Andrew paid an addition £79 for immunisation

www.ingramcontent.com/pod-product-compliance
Lightning Source LLC
Chambersburg PA
CBHW070100020526
44112CB00034B/2102